THE LEARNÈ
HIPPOPOTAMUS

Poems Conveying Useful Information About Animals
Ordinary and Extraordinary

GAVIN EWART

Illustrated by Ronald Ferns

HUTCHINSON
London Melbourne Auckland Johannesburg

For Jane, Funk and Ali Bongo

Copyright © Gavin Ewart 1986
Copyright © Illustrations Ronald Ferns 1986

ALL RIGHTS RESERVED

First published in 1986
by Hutchinson Children's Books
An imprint of Century Hutchinson Ltd
Brookmount House, 62–65 Chandos Place, Covent Garden,
London WC2N 4NW

Century Hutchinson Publishing Group (Australia) Pty Ltd
16–22 Church Street, Hawthorn, Melbourne, Victoria 3122

Century Hutchinson Group (NZ) Ltd
32–34 View Road, PO Box 40-086, Glenfield, Auckland 10

Century Hutchinson Group (SA) Pty Ltd
PO Box 337, Bergvlei 2012, South Africa

Designed by Philippa Bramson

Set in Caslon Old Face 2 Roman
Printed in Great Britain by Redwood Burn Ltd, Trowbridge, Wiltshire
and bound by Hunter and Foulis Ltd,
Edinburgh

British Library Cataloguing in Publication Data

Ewart, Gavin
    The learned hippopotamus: poems conveying
    useful information about animals ordinary and
    extraordinary.
    I. Title   II. Ferns, Ronald
    821'.912   PR6055.W3

    ISBN 0-09-163350-8

INTRODUCTION

All the creatures in this book, except for the Dogbird and the Sheepbird (both of which I made up) are real animals. They are described as they actually are or as they were (in the case of the Dinosaurs) in all their wonderful variety.

'Everything that lives is holy' wrote the English poet William Blake. It is up to us to respect and preserve the plants and animals – not to destroy them, for profit, by chemical sprays or too much hunting.

All these little poems are meant to be entertaining. And so are the pictures. Ronald Ferns and I hope you enjoy them.

GAVIN EWART

THE learnèd Hippopotamus
Uses long words like 'dichotomous' –
If they don't exist, he makes them up!
The true scholars and the highbrows
Raise their supercilious eyebrows
But he blows bubbles at them all – glug,
glug,
glup
and
glup!

THE Whale
Smacks the sea with its tail.
The sea doesn't mind being spanked – on
The contrary, it gives the whale plankton.

THE Agouti can jump, from a sitting start,
A distance of twenty feet.
He has nervous spasms
But he can leap chasms –
His jumping is hard to beat!

Note Agouti
Rhymes with snooty.
He lives in Mexico and the Argentine,
Where the green vegetation is particularly
fine!

IF you die in the desert, expect no sepulture!
You'll be swallowed down by the Bearded Vulture!
The Bearded Vulture or Lammergeier
Will strip you to pieces, layer by layer –
Dessert in the desert you'll be providing!
So stay safe at home, and be law-abiding!

Note The Bearded Vulture was called the
Lammergeier because it could carry off
lambs. Sepulture means burial.

THE Goose is the male,
The female's the Gander.
Geese get quite cross,
The Ganders are blander.

THE Slow Loris
Doesn't know about Liberals or Tories.
It lives in trees in Assam
And on the islands of Java, Sumatra and Borneo.
It comes out at night
And, very very slowly, it will climb.
It might vote Labour
If it could get to the Polling Station in time.

ALTHOUGH people make jokes
About fish fingers,
Everybody understands
That fish don't have hands.
They don't have feet either,
You'll never hear a fish's footfall.
But there actually *is* one fish
That can blow itself up like a football!

Note Known as the Puffer Fish or the Porcupine
Fish, it has spines and lives in tropical seas.
The blowing-up is to discourage predators.

IF you're a Bear
There's a lot of wear and tear.
You may be shot at now and then
By horrible men
Who drink beer and Coca-cola.

If you're the kind called Polar
You see nothing but snow and ice –
Which is not very nice.

THE Marsupial Mole
Is an underground animal,
As an overground animal
It's a failure.
It lives in the middle of South Australia.
Like princesses in the fairy stories
It has long silky golden-yellow hair.
It might not be exactly what you want
But scientists call it an aberrant polyprotodont.

Note 'Aberrant' means 'of an unusual type'.
Marsupials are very primitive animals, that
carry their young ones in pouches. The
kangaroo is the best-known example of this.

THAT loud hum in Sausalito
Isn't caused by a mosquito
Or anything that flies above –
But by fish, when they're in love!
Houseboat-dwellers have good reason
To know when it's the mating season –
Fun and games, and amorous sport!
California's famed resort
Gets more song than sleepers wish
From the Plain-finned Midshipman Fish!

News Item 'Scientists yesterday blamed courting
fish for a loud hum that for years has
kept houseboat dwellers awake in the
California resort of Sausalito . . .'
The Guardian,
22 August 1985

Never rely on a Lion.
He will eat the Eland and the Gazelle –
And he's perfectly willing to
Eat you as well!

THE Turtle
Is not like a racing car that can hurtle
Round corners, throwing up the sand –
He's not good on land.
He hasn't a clue, he hasn't a glimmer.
But he's a marvellous swimmer!

THE average Snake
Is as thin as a rake,
But a Python sometimes looks fat.
By adjusting its throat
It can swallow a goat,
Not to mention a dog or a cat.

It's a bit of a burden,
It's a bit of a load
Being a Toad!
People go round saying you're ugly and slimy –
But a Toad is clean, not dirty or grimy.
He has fascinating camouflage of blotches and
    mottles,
He eats the horrible flies and bluebottles.

If he tastes nasty, that's
Only so he doesn't get eaten by cats!

The Dogbird's barking
In the streets.
In the fields
The Sheepbird bleats,
Down among the
Bulls and cows.
But *everywhere*
The Catbird miaows!

Note The Dogbird and the Sheepbird are
      imagined, but the Catbird is real. It lives in
      the south of the USA, where it makes a
      noise like a cat.

SNOW-LEMMINGS in their summer phase
Are very round and brown —
Though they look rather sweet
They're not seen in the street
Or anywhere else in a town!

In winter they go purest white
And burrow under the snow —
They grow a big claw
On each digging paw
Every autumn (if you *must* know).

In South America you find the Puma,
Also in Mexico, where the great King Montezuma
Probably had a few as pets.
It's about three and a half feet long
Yet no wise person forgets
That if you do it wrong
It has no sense of humour . . .
If you give it a pat
It will purr like a cat
(But don't rely too much on *that*).

WASPS always look as though
They ought to be part of a football team.
But I wouldn't like to play them, even so,
With their stripey supporters waving and singing
And all that bad-tempered stinging!

EVERYONE knows a Flying Fox
Cannot be kept in a box.
He likes to feel free
And swoop about from tree to tree.
Much more remarkable than that,
He's really a kind of fruit-eating Bat.

NOBODY could look classier
Than the Tarsier.
Its eyes are simply enormous –
Quite different from the dormouse!

NEVER try to make your meals
From the big Electric Eels!
Slim, athletic, not fat-bellied,
Never try to serve them jellied!
You would be a laughing-stock –
And you'd get a frightful shock!

Note Jellied eels are still popular in London.

THE world is full of Elephants,
The baby ones and taller ones.
African Elephants have great big ears,
The Indian ones have smaller ones.

WHAT can a Herring do?
For deeds of derring-do
Its talents are small.
But it can swim in sea
So icy-cold that we
Wouldn't be choosing to,
We'd be refusing to
Swim there at all!

NEVER mix up Raccoons
With cocoons or macaroons.
They're absolutely different.
(They're nothing to do with butterflies or biscuits.)
They frisk about with long whiskers.
There are two different types
But they both have long bushy tails
With black and white stripes.

NEVER antagonise an Ant!
Every ant can crawl about
All over you and tickle you
Until you fall about.
And if you should *antagonise*
They'll give you dire ant agonies.
Some of them have wings,
Some can bite and some have stings.

THE Anteater
Isn't a small or a scant eater.
To keep going and in the pink
It has to eat many more ants than you might think!
To get to be really fit — and stay that way —
It has to eat hundreds of thousands a day!

Don't be frightened of Kangaroos –
They're not dangerous, or even *dangaroos*
But they certainly can hop!
About twenty feet when they're going flat out,
And when they get started
It's   hard   to
    very   them
         for
                  STOP!

EVERYBODY knows
That it's the Cock that crows.
If it were cleverer or more knowing
The *Crow* would do the crowing!

THE Ocelot
Is a kind of big fierce cat –
The kind you can't boss a lot!

It lives in Central
And South America.
It's never called Eric
Or Erica.

The idea of having one
As a pet
Is an idea
You'd better forget!

THE Katydid
Is a kind of flat green grasshopper
Found in America.
It makes a noise with its legs –
Katydid – Katydidn't – Katydid!
That's what it sounds like, they say.

But what Katy did or didn't do
Is a mystery to me and to you.
And it's unlikely the Katydid itself
Ever knew!

PORCUPINES
Are covered in horrible long spines,
They move slowly about
Looking bilious,
And the expression on their faces
Is always supercilious.

HIS father was a Tiger
And his mother was a Lion.
(He wasn't ever in Noah's Ark.)
No label you could tie on
Would make him less a miracle,
Quite special and quite rare.
And if you saw him in a zoo
You'd simply stand and stare!

Note Tigons can be bred in captivity. They don't
occur in the wild.

SOME Dinosaurs were heavily armoured,
Like tanks.
They walked around as safe
As money in banks.
If the big meat-eaters grabbed at their scales
They would hit them hard with their tails!

IF you see a Leopard
Wearing a leotard,
Hiding in the trees,
You'll know at once that he
Can't tell his T's from P's!

Not many people are really inspired
To learn the names of all the Dinosaurs –
It can make you quite tired.
But everybody's heard of Tyrannosaurus Rex,
Just as everybody's heard of sex.

There's one with a very knowing look,
Called Kannemeyeria.
It knows that trying to spell its name
Will make you much wearier!

Sparrows are very chirpy –
They've never heard of Euterpě
(The Ancient Greek Muse of Lyric Verse).
But at least it's no worse.
No sparrow is the kind of uneducated twerp
That goes around pronouncing her Euterp!

A really hot meal
Doesn't appeal
To a Seal.
Its favourite dish
Is very cold fish!

THE Flamingo is very highbrow.
It scorns pop music, football and bingo.
It would like to be a famous Italian tenor
Called Flaccido Flamingo.

STOP *badgering me!*
Is a cry one hears
(But not from Badgers).
Badgers are beautiful
And not curmudgeons or cadgers.
They're never red or blue or green.
They stick to black and white –
And they only come out at night.

No *sensible* little swimmers wish
To meet the deceitful Angler Fish!
It very nastily lies in wait.
Fish must avoid the tempting bait
Waved on a rod above its head!
If not, they'll very soon be dead!

James James
Willoughby Wallaby
Lived in the Adelaide Zoo.
He had deep deep thoughts
(For a wallaby)
Though he was only two.

James James
Didn't like being a wallaby
(*They* are an undersized crew),
He longed to be
Not just a wallaby
But a big kangaroo!

James James
Willoughby Wallaby
Said to this mother (in Strine*):
'If I could only
Be a big kangaroo
That'd be fair dinkum and fine!'

James James
Willoughby's mother
Said: 'You never can be
A duck-billed platypus,
Koala or anything
Else in this land of the free!'

James James
Willoughby Wallaby
Sobbed and felt truly depressed!
But his mother consolingly
Said 'Being a wallaby
Is *always* considered the best!'

James James
Thought, as she cuddled him,
'I can't be a kangaroo
But I *don't mind*.
I'm the best-loved wallaby
In the whole of the Adelaide Zoo!'

*'Strine' is 'Australian', referring to the local
accent. There is a very famous poem by A. A.
Milne, on which this poem is based. 'Fair
dinkum' means 'very good indeed'. A wallaby is a
good deal smaller than a kangaroo.

MANY stories are told of the wily Opossum!
The Americans, who really know 'em
Say: Don't trust 'em further than you can toss 'em,
Don't trust 'em further than you can throw 'em!
These are the Common Opossums, but there are also
Four-eyed Opossums, Mouse-Opossums, Woolly
    Opossums.
They can all hang down from trees by their tails
Like big furry blossoms.

But beware the Water Opossum or Yapok!
It has a terrible smell.
When the Indians of Brazil come across it
They retreat with a yell!

Note The Four-eyed Opossum hasn't got four
    eyes; but it does have two white spots, one
    above each eye, which give this impression.

THE gaudy Parrot Fish
Can't talk or scream,
It wanders round all day
As if in a dream.

But perhaps it's saying something
That we can't hear?
The other fish don't pay much attention
As they hover near.

If it's saying 'Who's a pretty boy, then?'
It must be very boring.
Perhaps all the other fish
Are fast asleep and snoring?

THE Whippoorwill is a bird
Whose song in Britain
Is very seldom heard.
In fact, if you wanted to be
A bit more clever,
Instead of 'seldom'
You could say 'never'!

The notes of the song
Are supposed to sound like
'Whip poor Will!'
Perhaps they do
In the Deep South of the USA,
Though that seems a silly thing
For any bird to say.

WHITE men in Africa,
Puffing at their pipes,
Think the zebra's a white horse
With black stripes.

Black men in Africa,
With pipes of different types,
Know the Zebra's a black horse
With white stripes.

THINKING about the Ichthyosaurus
Would never send us to sleep or bore us –
It was a huge great fish with flippers,
About as big as 50,000 kippers.
Over and above all this – or, rather, underneath –
Its nose was long and sharp, and it had hundreds of
    teeth.

It rushed about in the warm seas
In a time when there were no birds or bees
And people hadn't yet been invented.
If you saw one you would think you were demented
Because of the really terrific and frightening size
Of its huge great deadly prehistoric eyes.

MANY people are very fond of a Donkey –
Though some say it's just a horse that's gone
   wonky.

THE Ring-Tailed Lemur
Is in no way a plotter or a schemer.
Nor is it Lancastrian or a Lascar.
It lives quite happily with fruit bats and scarlet
   frogs
And things called tenrecs that look like hedgehogs.
It won't live anywhere but Madagascar!
It likes the climate
And, as we are, it's definitely a primate!

Note Lancastrians come from Lancashire,
        Lascars are Indian sailors. Primates are the
        highest class of creature, like men and the
        apes.

THE Octopus is an animal that has eight feet.
If it didn't have eight feet it wouldn't be complete.
But what nobody really and truly understands
Is that the octopus regards them as *hands*.

SHAKESPEARE wrote:
'The harmless necessary Cat'.
But mice and rats (for example)
Don't see it exactly like that.